IMAGES OF ENGLAND

CENTRAL BIRMINGHAM
1950-1980

IMAGES OF ENGLAND

CENTRAL BIRMINGHAM
1950-1980

MARTIN HAMPSON

Frontispiece: The Alpha Tower rising over the Gas Street Basin and the site of the future James Brindley pub in 1972.

First published by Tempus in 2004

Reprinted in 2017 by

The History Press
The Mill, Brimscombe Port,
Stroud, Gloucestershire, GL5 2QG
www.thehistorypress.co.uk

British Library Cataloguing in Publication Data.
A catalogue record for this book is available from the British Library.

ISBN 978 0 7524 3361 5

Typesetting and origination by Tempus Publishing Limited.
Printed in Great Britain.

Contents

Acknowledgements

I am grateful to Birmingham Library Services for allowing me to use their photographs. All the images come from collections in the Local Studies and History Department of the Central Library and were taken mainly by council staff in the Public Works and City Engineer's departments. I am, in addition, grateful to Mrs Betty Wright for permission to use five photographs taken by her late husband Donald (shown on pages 58, 59 and 76b). Finally, I am grateful to my former colleague, Keith Turner, for the fine example set by his previous books on Central Birmingham, and to Local Studies staff for technical advice.

Smallbrook Ringway, now the Queensway, *c.* 1965.

Introduction

For a city like Birmingham, whose motto is 'Forward', change has been a fact of life for a long time. As early as 1828, the comedian James Dobbs was lamenting the speed of change in his ballad, 'I can't find Brummagem', and there was certainly major rebuilding and new development in both the eighteenth and nineteenth centuries. The new town of Georgian terraces, rising on the hilltop round St Philip's, must have seemed a radical innovation, like the late Victorian creation of two civic squares and the driving of Corporation Street through the worst of the central slums.

In 1950, the city centre would still have been recognisable to an Edwardian. In spite of bomb damage and some individual new buildings, the basic street pattern remained the same; the Bull Ring's open market still sloped down from the High Street to St Martin's, as it had done for centuries. Trams still trundled down Victorian shopping streets lined with specialised family businesses. Steam trains still halted at cavernous, soot-blackened stations, their passengers emerging to patronise shops and cafés, pubs and hotels, some little changed in decades. Photographs of the period suggest that it was a bustling regional centre at the heart of the transport network yet still functioning on a recognisably human scale.

Major changes were on the way. As soon as funds permitted, the major 'Big Top' bomb site was reconstructed, providing 1950s Birmingham with its first purpose-built shopping and office complex, including a high-rise block. Notably innovative for the time, with its service tunnel and modern arcades providing a streamlined version of the bombed originals, it foreshadowed on a smaller scale the Bull Ring of a decade later.

Many post-war changes were planned in the 1930s and were merely delayed by the war. Traffic was already considered a problem in the 1920s, and a one-way system had been in operation since 1933. The Inner Ring Road, discussed as early as 1917, was being reconsidered in 1943. In some ways a very 1930s concept, having seven main junctions with incoming arterial roads and large traffic islands, it was intended to divert through traffic from the city centre, and was designed primarily as a traffic road, with few shop, office or warehouse frontages. Begun in 1957 with Smallbrook Ringway, its most successful section, it took fourteen years to build.

Sir Herbert Manzoni, the motive force behind the Ring Road and associated redevelopment, was the City Engineer and Surveyor from 1935 to 1963, and most of his plans were already on the drawing board by the late 1930s. He made use of legislation in the Housing Act of 1936, which made provision for the defining of redevelopment areas. Five inner suburbs were chosen for total clearance and rebuilding: Duddeston and Nechells, Newtown, Highgate, Lee Bank, and Ladywood. Redevelopment areas were based on a system of strict zoning that separated land into areas of housing, industry and open space. Neighbourhoods were to include a community centre and shopping facilities. Material and labour shortages delayed work on the first area, Duddeston and Nechells, until the early 1950s.

The Inner Ring Road was allied to a similar city centre development of over 1,200 acres, again with zoning. The building of the Ring Road would in itself involve much demolition and rebuilding, obliterating old street patterns and sweeping aside all in its path – an impact not unlike that of Victorian railways.

Once described as an engineer's solution rather than an architect's, the building of the Ring Road successfully eased traffic flow and separated pedestrians from vehicles. However, it also broke up communities, divided the Gun Quarter in half, and limited pedestrian access to districts beyond the Ring Road that could now be reached only by subway. Most importantly, the showpiece Bull Ring Centre, whose covered shopping malls were the first of their kind in Europe, suffered from the start from complex pedestrian access, being built around the Ring Road and reached on five different levels. The Ring Road effectively cut off St Martin's and the open market from the city centre.

Manzoni's uncompromising espousal of a new beginning, although in tune with post-war thinking, was already being modified by the late 1960s when the first steps towards canal redevelopment started with the construction of James Brindley Walk. Here, there was a successful blending of old and new; the modern tower flats co-existed beside both restored canal-side cottages and a brand-new pub that used a traditional narrowboat as a summer bar. This development not only reaffirmed city centre living but emphasised the leisure and tourist potential of the canal network whose industrial base was in decline. The later, much more ambitious Brindleyplace, clearly owed much to this comparatively small beginning. In much the same way, the establishment of several early nightclubs near the canals was a harbinger of the much later major Broad Street developments.

The early 1970s marked further significant changes, such as the first experiments in pedestrianization in streets such as Union Street and Cherry Street; this was later adopted on a bigger scale in New Street and elsewhere. Allied to this increasingly pedestrian-friendly approach was the physical enhancement of several streets by the preservation of attractive period façades, notably on Waterloo Street, where several Georgian office blocks were totally modernised internally while retaining their original frontages. This practice was later adopted comprehensively on New Street and Colmore Row, showing that modernisation and conservation could work together.

It was inevitable that successful pedestrianization would lead to modification of the Inner Ring Road itself and, by the late 1980s, Paradise Circus was being lowered and spanned by a new pedestrian bridge. The 'concrete collar' which had confined the city centre for a generation was ceremonially breached in Great Charles Street, and even the showpiece Smallbrook Queensway eventually saw its subway replaced by a pedestrian crossing, improving access to the Hurst Street entertainment quarter.

The bridge at Paradise Circus literally led the way to later developments of international significance such as Centenary Square and the Convention Centre. Only by loosening the 'concrete collar' was the great success of Broad Street and Brindleyplace achievable. The Inner Ring Road survives in modified form; like many 1960s achievements it was a bold idea but needed some reworking. Two redeveloped inner suburbs are being substantially rebuilt again – a further 'new beginning'. In the cycle of change, the 1960s Bull Ring may be seen as a 'trial run' for its present, more successful, replacement, with direct access to the city again restored.

It is the aim of this book to show the varied scenes and concerns of three decades when the foundations of present-day Birmingham were laid.

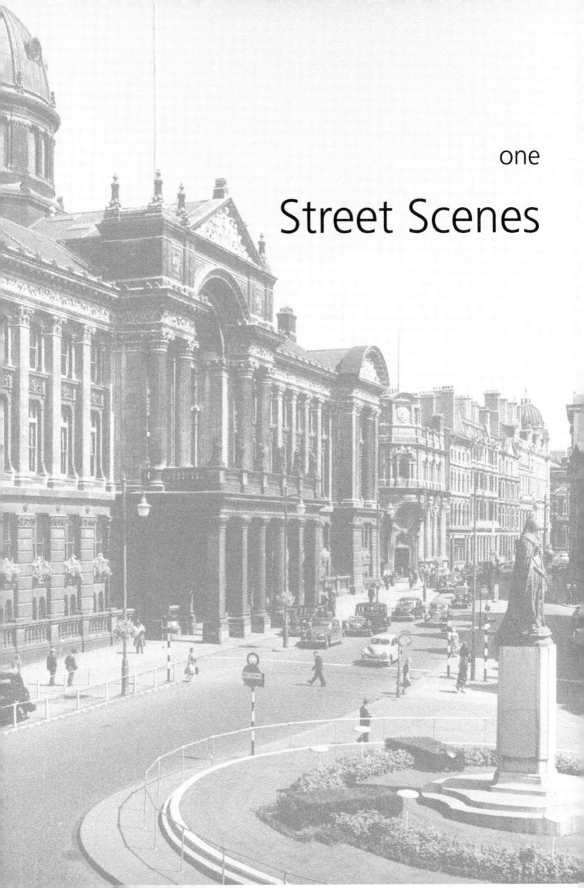

one

Street Scenes

The junction of New Street and Corporation Street in 1964 shows the then offices of the *Birmingham Post & Mail*. In the block to the left, the Kardomah Café, a favourite meeting place with its fine Arts and Crafts interior, can be seen adjoining Austin Reed.

Burlington passage, seen here in 1953, links New Street with Lower Temple Street, and passes beneath the Midland Hotel. It survives in modified form following the rebuilding of the hotel (now the Burlington).

Above: New Street, *c.* 1950. This photograph shows King Edward House (built on the original site of King Edward's school), which contained at the time both C&A and Littlewoods.

Left: Looking in the window of Day's shoe shop near Piccadilly Arcade in New Street, *c.* 1950.

The New Street arcade, looking towards City Arcade, *c.* 1965. It is a 1950s rebuilding of the original Victorian arcade which was bombed in 1941. It forms part of the Big Top site, so called because following the bombing it remained for some years an open space used for circuses and other outdoor entertainments.

Smallbrook Ringway (later Queensway) in 1964, looking towards the new Bull Ring Centre. The bridge provided direct access between New Street station and the Bull Ring.

Union Street in 1972, looking towards High Street and the Big Top site (on the right), with the Martineau Square development (on the left), which was completed by 1962.

In 1973, Union Street saw an early, successful experiment in pedestrianization. Such a people-friendly approach provided a striking contrast to the previous decade when pedestrians were more likely to be relegated to a subway.

Colmore Row, in about 1956, looking towards Steelhouse Lane.

Colmore Row, c. 1960. The photograph shows the Grand Hotel, the old Snow Hill station and Steelhouse Lane shortly before the Colmore Circus reconstruction. Most of Colmore Row's late Victorian frontages still survive, even though there has been much rebuilding behind the facades. Still one of Central Birmingham's finest streets, the Row narrowly escaped demolition and incorporation into the Inner Ring Road scheme.

Newhall Street in 1963, looking towards Colmore Row. The road follows the line of the drive to New Hall, former home of the Colmore family, the local landowners.

Snow Hill in 1959, showing a variety of small specialised family businesses, destined soon to disappear in the wake of the Inner Ring Road.

Cherry Street in 1972, looking towards the Cathedral churchyard, with Rackhams (now House of Fraser) on the right.

The newly pedestrianized Cherry Street in 1973. The street stands on the site of a former cherry orchard.

Above: A Georgian terrace on Temple Row in 1954 is a reminder of how fashionable residential parts of the city centre once were (a trend being recently revived). Before its late Victorian rebuilding as a business centre, nearby Colmore Row was home to many prosperous merchants and manufacturers.

Right: Like nearby Union Street and Cherry Street, Temple Row was pedestrianized by 1974. A variety of street furniture helped to discourage unauthorised drivers.

Above: Shoppers are seen here sitting in the shelter on Temple Row in front of Rackhams in 1973.

Left: This image of the High Street in the early 1950s shows the corner leading down to the Bull Ring with some property marked out for redevelopment. The tall building in the background is Times Furnishing (now Waterstone's).

Opposite below: The Great Western arcade, *c.* 1955. This arcade links Colmore Row and Temple Row. Completed by William Ward in 1876, it follows the line of the tunnel to Snow Hill station. Its stylish, specialised shops still provide an attractive alternative to the larger chain stores. Partially reconstructed after wartime bombing, it was further refurbished in the 1980s in a modified Victorian style.

Above: This photograph of the High Street in 1971 shows the Big Top block, seen on the left. Built between 1955 and 1961 on a bombed and long vacant site, like much early post-war reconstruction, it seems architecturally rather bland, but functions well as a shop and office complex, with a modern rebuilding of the original arcades and an underground service tunnel. It was the city's first purpose-built shopping centre.

Above: The North Western Arcade, *c.* 1964. It is a continuation of the Great Western Arcade, linking Temple Row to Corporation Street, and still following the line of Snow Hill tunnel. Originally opened in 1884, it was rebuilt following the expiration of the original seventy-five-year lease.

Left: The photograph of Victoria Square in around 1956 shows Queen Victoria's statue on its original traffic island with the Council House on the left, and, beyond it, a number of the *palazzo*-style offices still characteristic of Colmore Row.

Left: At the point of change in 1971, this view from a pigeon-marked pillar of the Town Hall shows Galloway's Corner in Victoria Square shortly before its demolition. Named after Gordon Galloway's chemist and camera shop, this block embodied the ever-changing Birmingham street scene, since it was itself a replacement of the demolished Christ Church (of which only Christ Church Steps now survive). Although the plan to widen Colmore Row (which motivated the demolition) was later abandoned, the opening up of Victoria Square paved the way for the 1990s improvements, with fountains, cascades and statues.

A tram passes down Corporation Street in 1950 with Queen's Hotel and Midland Bank, now another Waterstone's, in the background. The Queen's Hotel fronted New Street station until 1965.

The junction of Corporation Street and Martineau Street in 1950 with the site of the present House of Fraser and the entrance to the original North Western arcade on the left. Beyond the tram rises Lewis's, with its sunblinds, while the tall thin tower of Central Hall closes the view.

The junction of Corporation Street and Martineau Street in 1952. Following the expiration of seventy-five-year leases, the whole of Martineau Street was closed in 1960 and the site up to Union Street developed as the Martineau Square precinct.

One of Birmingham's finest townscapes is still provided by the view at the northern end of Corporation Street where the redbrick and terracotta Victoria Law Courts (built in 1891) are perfectly complemented by the Methodist Central Hall (built in 1903). These outstanding examples of Birmingham's redbrick Gothic style of building form a monumental 'gateway' through which the central fire station and University of Aston buildings can be seen. This view was taken around 1970, just before the major roadworks at Lancaster Circus, straight ahead.

A view towards the General Hospital at the junction of Corporation Street and Steelhouse Lane, *c.* 1952.

Above: Gosta Green in 1950 with the former Delicia cinema (then a wrestling venue) straight ahead and the Sacks of Potatoes pub on the right.

Left: Steelhouse Lane, *c.* 1952. This photograph looks towards Snow Hill station, with the Wesleyan Assurance building behind the tram and the Gaumont cinema on the far right. In 1963, as part of the Inner Ring Road scheme, the huge traffic roundabout known as Colmore Circus was constructed. This left the cinema and insurance offices stranded above a large pedestrian underpass. These two remaining buildings were later demolished, the Wesleyan being rebuilt in 1988. In a further redevelopment, the 'hole in the ground' was recently filled in.

The junction of Snow Hill and Steelhouse Lane in 1962, shortly before these corner buildings were demolished as part of the Inner Ring Road scheme. On the far left is Snow Hill station with the Wesleyan Assurance block rising on the right.

Digbeth High Street in 1955 shortly after the road was widened. This street was one of the earliest in Birmingham to be adapted to post-war traffic needs, the whole of one side being demolished and rebuilt (as later on Bristol Street), as part of the conversion to dual carriageway.

The junction of Horse Fair and Holloway Head in 1960 with the old church of St Catherine of Siena (built in 1875) on the left.

This photograph of Bristol Street in 1960 shows the route to the city centre, just before major reconstruction work began not only on the road itself but on housing on both sides.

Right: Edmund Street, *c.* 1955. The photograph shows the old central library on the left and Mason College (the original university) on the right. The huge building straight ahead is West End Chambers, on Broad Street, used latterly by the Britannic Assurance Co. and now the site of Alpha Tower.

Below: This image shows the junction of Easy Row and Broad Street in 1958 with Suffolk Street straight ahead. On the left are several terraces of Georgian office buildings converted from former town houses, while the tall West End Chambers block adjoins the site of the former canal basin and Birmingham Canal Navigation offices. None of the buildings in this picture now survive. Paradise Circus occupies the left-hand site.

Above: Looking up Broad Street in 1973 with the site of the present Centenary Square and Convention Centre straight ahead. The recently constructed pedestrian subways are visible in the foreground and, beyond the dome of the Hall of Memory, is a Georgian industrial terrace. Between this block and the new Repertory Theatre to the right is a large dark gable belonging to Bingley Hall (built in 1850), one of the country's earliest purpose-built exhibition centres. The opening of the National Exhibition Centre in 1976 hastened its closure, and the International Convention Centre was officially opened on the site in 1991.

Until the construction of Centenary Square in 1989, extensive gardens stretched between Baskerville House and Bingley Hall, of which this fountain (seen in 1954) was one of the attractions.

Above: Shops towards the top of Broad Street in 1957 with the large block of Kunzles' cake and chocolate factory visible to the right. At this time, Broad Street still had a large number of small specialised shops.

Opposite below: Baskerville House and the Hall of Memory, *c.* 1957. This was the only part of a large Civic Centre planned in 1934 that was actually completed. The Planning Department was based here for some years.

Left: The Crescent in Cambridge Street is seen here in 1964, shortly before demolition. It formed part of a speculator's plan, drawn up in 1788, for twenty-three Georgian houses on the edge of town. Due to a recession, only twelve houses were built; the economic recovery brought with it new factories, discouraging further residential interest. The Crescent Theatre Co. originally used a house here, hence their name. The Crescent project formed part of an early, unsuccessful attempt by Birmingham to reinvent itself as a fashionable resort.

Broad Street in 1973 showing the Crown Inn (later Edward's and Reflex), and the Church of the Messiah, built over the canal. On the far right are the remains of the former Prince of Wales Theatre, which was bombed during the war and later incorporated into Bingley Hall (itself demolished in the late 1980s to make way for the Convention Centre).

The junction of Bath Row and Wheeleys Lane in 1960 shortly before the redevelopment of the whole area.

A 1959 view of Bath Row with the ruined church of St Thomas, which was completed by Thomas Rickman in 1829 and destroyed by wartime bombs. The gardens were originally laid out to commemorate the Queen's Coronation, but were transformed into a Peace Garden in association with the laying out of Centenary Square (1989). The loggia which formed part of the original Civic Centre development on Broad Street was rebuilt here.

Shops on Islington Row, near Five Ways, in 1958, shortly before redevelopment.

Lee Bank Road in 1960, showing the kind of shabby, run-down housing which invited comprehensive replacement in several inner-city areas.

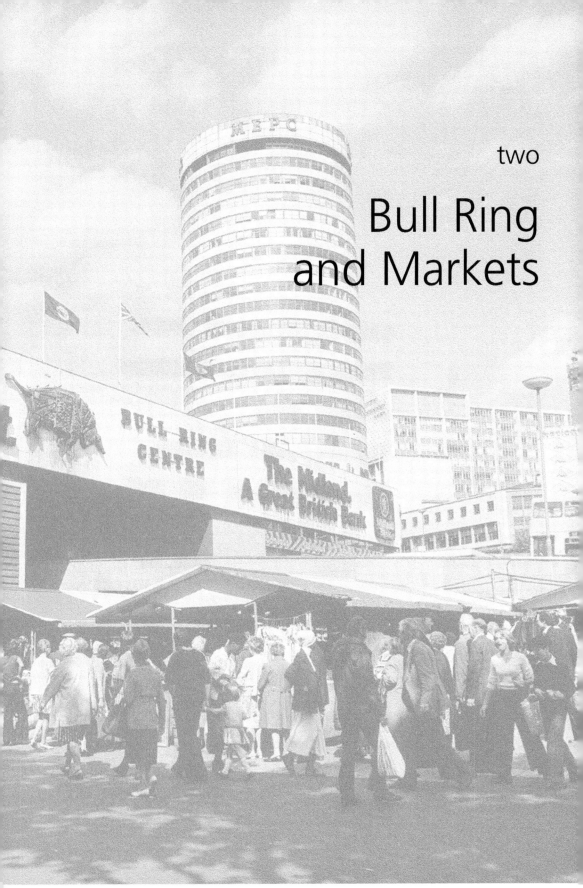

two

Bull Ring
and Markets

An aerial view of Digbeth High Street taken in 1953, looking towards the coach station (marked by parked buses) and the wholesale markets area, in the top left of the photograph. At this time, Digbeth still looked much as it had done immediately after the war, although as early as 1935, Parliamentary approval had been given for the compulsory purchase of land for building dual carriageways. Furthermore, the Inner Ring Road scheme had been conceived as early as 1917. Financial restrictions were finally relaxed sufficiently, however, for Digbeth's road widening to be implemented by 1955. This paved the way for the Inner Ring Road, the construction of which was started in 1957. The Inner Ring Road was a catalyst for the rebuilding of the Bull Ring and its associated wholesale markets.

In 1973, shortly before comprehensive redevelopment of the wholesale markets area, the city's Public Works Department made a detailed survey of the streets and individual buildings that were doomed to disappear. This picture shows the junction of Jamaica Row and Bromsgrove Street.

This 1973 view of Sherlock Street East shows the number of small family businesses which operated alongside the large wholesale market complexes.

The junction of Jamaica Row and Sherlock Street East in 1973, looking left towards Smithfield Market.

Upper Dean Street in 1973.

The junction of Bradford Street and Sherlock Street East in 1973, showing the meat market and, on the right, the Birmingham Arms, one of several famous market pubs lost to the redevelopment.

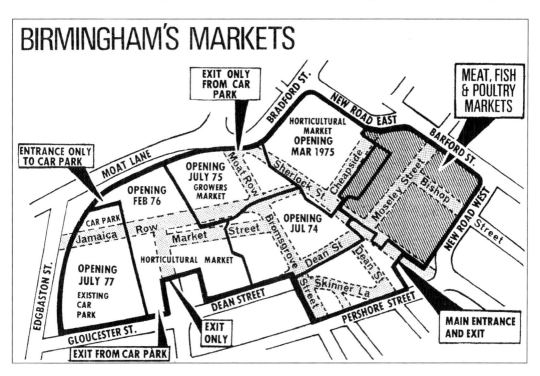

Plan for the proposed redevelopment of the wholesale markets area, showing how, bar the replacement of individual buildings, the whole street pattern was to be changed.

Work begins on the wholesale markets site, *c.* 1972.

The High Street slopes down towards St Martin's church on a showery day, *c.* 1957. This image shows the gables of St Martin's Hotel beside the church and the pillars of the old Market Hall rising on the right. The open market square presented a timeless scene, tracing its functions directly back to 1166 when the first market charter was awarded. The Bull Ring, however, had been bombed in 1940 when the Market Hall was burned out; this encouraged plans for post-war redevelopment.

Shoppers wander through the open market in 1954. Post-war proposals were not all for comprehensive redevelopment. It was suggested by some, for instance, that the Market Hall be retained and re-roofed, whilst others argued for keeping at least the open market intact and its immediate setting unchanged.

This photograph, taken in 1967, presents a telling contrast with the two preceding scenes. While the new Inner Ring Road remains at ground level, the market has been relegated to a hole in the ground, accessible from the city centre only by pedestrian subway. St Martin's House, the office block on the left, also lacks the human, domestic scale of the previous Bull Ring buildings.

Right: The new Bull Ring Centre and
St Martin's church, *c.* 1970. This picture
clearly shows how successfully the Inner
Ring Road scheme segregated traffic
and pedestrians, and also how effectively
it separated St Martin's and the historical
markets of Birmingham, from the
remainder of the city.

Below: The Bull Ring centre and open
market in 1963. Described as 'one of the
most important shopping centres yet
built in this country' by Pevsner in
1966, the centre was designed by
Sydney Greenwood and T.J. Hirst while
the open market and associated buildings
(Rotunda and St Martin's House) were
by James A. Roberts. Constructed
between 1961 and 1964, the open
market covered a 3-acre site and
included a retail market, two levels of
shops, a multi-storey car park, a multi-
storey office block, and a bus terminal.

The indoor fish market, also in 1963. While built to a design already familiar in America, the Bull Ring centre was uncommon for the time in being centrally located rather than in an outer suburb. It was also unusual for the architects' skilful handling of a very complex site, bisected by two wide carriageways and with entrances on five different levels.

Inside the new shopping centre, c. 1964. The open-plan malls can be seen as a modern development from Victorian shopping arcades. The bright décor and piped music proved particularly attractive to younger people, as did the novel approaches to the centre, ranging from New Street's open-air escalator (Britain's first), to the glazed bridge over the Manzoni Gardens linking New Street station to the Bull Ring. Traffic and pedestrians were totally separated throughout.

This photograph of the Bull Ring from St Martin's in 1975 shows the balcony used by public speakers in a long-standing local tradition (seen on the left). The Inner Ring Road can be seen running above the market stalls – a feature which has been reversed in the latest reconstruction of the Bull Ring where the road has been lowered and a new pedestrian approach to the High Street has been built over it. The 1960s setting of St Martin's was attractively landscaped, many mature churchyard trees being retained.

The Bull Ring centre and open market in 1978. Note how perfectly the circular hilltop Rotunda pulls together the disparate rectangular blocks of the main development.

The open market, *c.* 1978. It is still a popular local shopping destination.

The Manzoni Gardens, built on the site of the demolished market hall, were named after Sir Herbert Manzoni, the City Engineer and Surveyor between 1935 and 1963, and a pioneer of comprehensive redevelopment in the city and inner suburbs. Ironically the gardens vanished in the latest Bull Ring reconstruction – perhaps appropriately, in view of Manzoni's stated opinion that nothing need be built to last for more than twenty years.

Above: St Martin's House and car park, seen in 1972, were designed by James A. Roberts and completed in 1961. Although this uninspired office block won an award at the time, it was demolished as part of the second Bull Ring redevelopment in 2000, the car park having been declared unsafe in the early 1990s. The most memorable feature of St Martin's House was the large illuminated advertisement on the Moor Street side that adorned the night sky for many years.

Left: The Rotunda, completed by James A. Roberts in 1965, is probably the most memorable of the city centre's 1960s buildings. A twenty-four-storey cylindrical office block crowning the hill above the Bull Ring, it rises 271ft from a concrete base 54ft deep, making dramatic use of a confined site. Seen here soon after completion, it narrowly escaped demolition during recent redevelopment, and is now to be converted to luxury apartments, a fitting outcome for a valued, inspiring symbol of post-war Birmingham.

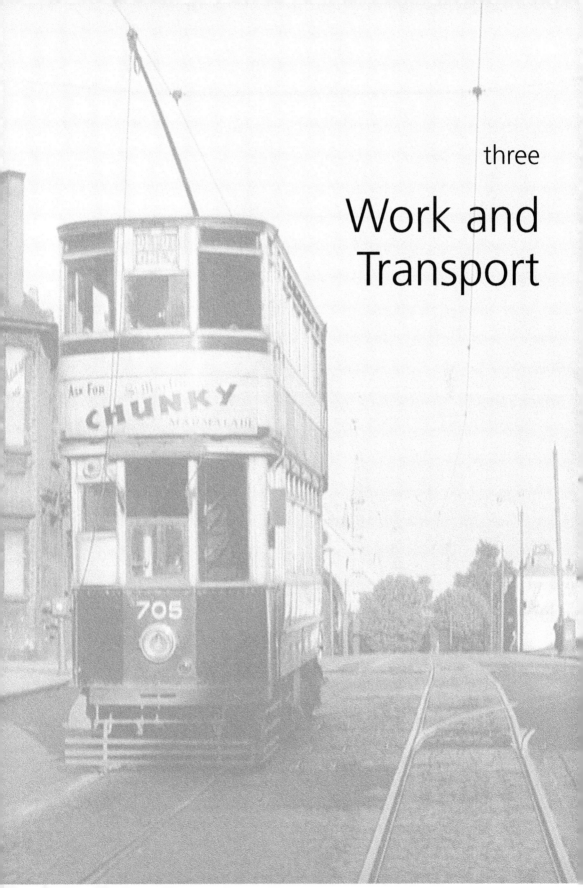

three

Work and Transport

Left: Day's distinctive Art Deco shoe shop, seen here in about 1950, was a prominent New Street landmark for many years.

Below: The interior of Day's shoe shop, *c.* 1950.

Grosvenor House completed for Shell-Mex BP by Cotton, Ballard and Blow in 1953, was the first new building erected on a bombed site in the city centre. Strikingly original with its strongly contrasting spikes, sharp angles and smooth curves, its eleven storeys made it a high-rise building for its time. It contained both an internal telephone system and compressed air tubes for sending messages.

Rackhams store on Corporation Street, seen here shortly after its completion by T.P. Bennett in 1961, was a landmark building of the period, and is the largest department store to survive from then. Its plain, geometric style, with zigzag elevations of blue fascia panels as the main decorative feature, was no doubt in harmony with the new-look fashions and furnishings of the time, which were also inside.

The *Birmingham Post & Mail* building on Colmore Circus was completed by John Madin in 1965 and is seen here in 1975. Like the Rotunda, it was an inspiring embodiment of post–war optimism. The long, low main block of four storeys is for newspaper production, with the sixteen-floor tower block let as offices. With the Ringway Centre (by John Madin's contemporary James Roberts), it can claim to be a leading landmark of the Inner Ring Road development.

Above: William Doubleday's building on Temple Row was built for the Staffordshire Bank in 1887. It was later used by the Bank of England as seen here, and has been rebuilt twice since 1970 – a not uncommon Birmingham phenomenon. It now houses the Bank of Scotland. The photograph here was taken in 1958.

Left: Bush House was originally started in 1937 as a training centre for Odeon cinemas; but the war intervened and the structure remained as a steel framework until 1956, when work recommenced and it was rumoured that Woolworths would complete the building. Seen here shortly after completion in around 1957, it became the City Housing Department; when it opened a year later, it was reputedly the largest of its kind in Europe. It was demolished in 1990 to make way for the Novotel development.

Left: The radar control room at Steelhouse Lane police station, *c.* 1953.

Below: The duty office at Steelhouse Lane, seen here in around 1955, was run by women police officers.

Opposite above: A chance encounter on Aston Street in Gosta Green, *c.* 1955.

Opposite below: Roadworks on Constitution Hill in 1972. The tall triangular terracotta and redbrick building is the Red Palace, built in 1896 as a memorial to Lord Roberts of Kandahar, and now a restaurant.

The tram terminus on Martineau Street in 1950.

The tram terminus on Steelhouse Lane in 1950.

The Navigation Street tram terminus, for Rednal and the Lickeys, with the original Matthew Boulton Technical College rising on the right, again in 1950.

A tram passing down Bradford Street on its final journey on 4 July 1953; it was headed for scrapping as this was the last day that trams ran in Birmingham.

Above: Removing tramlines on Bristol Street, looking towards the city centre, in 1953.

Opposite above: Children looking at model trams at the old Museum of Science and Industry in Newhall Street in 1973.

Opposite below: A trolleybus on the High Street in 1950.

54

The Midland Red bus station, opened as part of the new Bull Ring development in 1963. At the time of this photograph in 1967, there were also plans for a Corporation bus station at Paradise Circus but this was never finished. Although completely covered and with direct access to the shopping centre and markets, the Bull Ring station did not wear well, being latterly perceived as gloomy, seedy and claustrophobic. It closed in 1999, in preparation for the total rebuilding of the centre.

The junction of Digbeth High Street and Smithfield Street in 1953, showing the kind of traffic congestion that soon led to the widening of the High Street.

The Camp Hill flyover, seen here in 1961 soon after its erection, was an early local attempt to ease traffic congestion. Although now demolished, it can be seen as a small-scale precursor of later, more ambitious schemes at Masshouse Circus and Lancaster Circus.

Moor Street station in 1951 with a poster offering day trips to Stratford-upon-Avon for 3s 6d.

The booking hall at Snow Hill station in the 1960s, showing the clock which was a favourite meeting place for many years. Snow Hill was soon to lose its main-line status. Although there had been plans to rebuild Snow Hill as early as the 1930s, British Rail decided to rebuild New Street instead in connection with the West Coast Main Line electrification scheme.

Platform 6 at Snow Hill in 1965. During the rebuilding of New Street station, Snow Hill enjoyed an Indian summer with many main-line diversions. Appearances were deceptive, however, since there had been a general lack of maintenance since the war and much of the station had become structurally unsound.

The twilight of steam, with a goods train at Snow Hill in 1965. Main-line services ceased in 1967 and the main terminal building was demolished in 1970.

The lines at Snow Hill, looking towards Hockley. Although even local services had ceased by the early 1970s, the track-bed to Wolverhampton was retained in case of future need for rapid transit purposes. This foresight was justified, the station being reopened in 1987 with modest modern buildings and a track much simplified compared with this 1960s view. The Midland Metro tram service to Wolverhampton now operates alongside conventional rail services.

New Street station in 1952.

The South Wales Borderer steaming through New Street station on 20 July 1961.

The electrification of the West Coast Main Line coincided with British Rail's plans to rebuild New Street station which had been badly bombed during the war. The final plan, finished in 1964, featured a concrete raft over the station with a shopping arcade, office block and car park above, seen here in 1975.

The shopping centre above the station (now the Pallasades) is seen in 1979 with the many-jetted fountain then a popular focal point.

Above: Gas Street Basin in 1971, looking towards Broad Street, with the spire of the Church of the Messiah on the left and the disused Crown Brewery and former Pearce and Cutler glassworks closing the centre view. At this time, the tourist and recreational potential of the city's canals was just being realised. Some early nightclubs, like the Rum Runner and the Opposite Lock, bordered the canals, which were celebrated in the Cliff Richard film *Take Me High* (1973) as an appropriate setting for a restaurant.

Above: Working on the canal at Snow Hill in 1971.

Right: Walking beside the canal at Snow Hill in 1977.

Opposite below: Looking towards Gas Street Basin in 1958, showing the rather run-down, post-industrial setting which characterised the central canals until well into the 1960s. The Convention Centre now occupies the left-hand bank, whilst the Sea Life Centre and Brindleyplace are on the right-hand side.

Above: One of the most imaginative and positive changes of the late 1960s was the replacement of derelict workshops and warehouses by the James Brindley Walk and Civic Centre flats overlooking the canal. The centrepiece was the Longboat pub (seen here in 1975), where a real narrowboat moored beneath it was used as a floating bar in the summer. The modern tower flats were nicely contrasted with restored canal-side cottages; both brought back residential life to the city centre.

Left: Farmer's Locks looking towards Newhall Street and the old Science Museum in 1980.

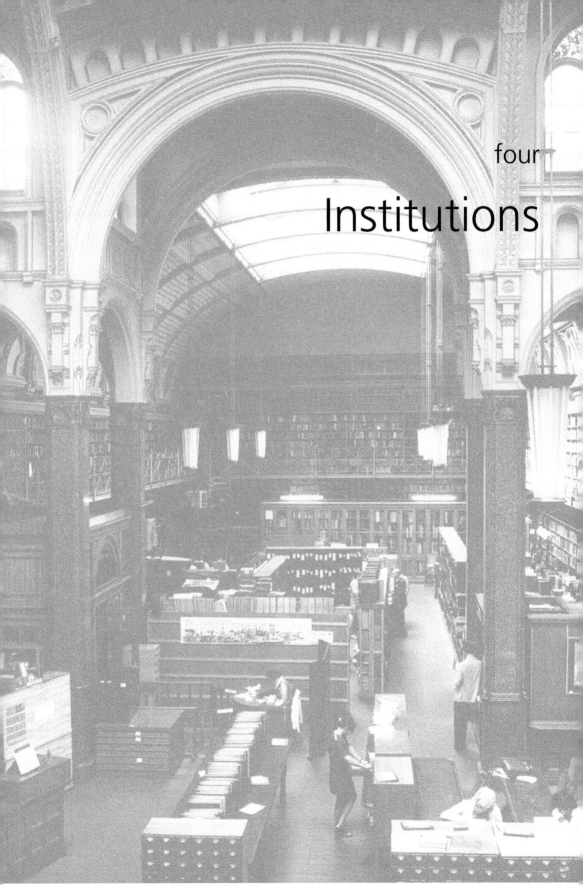

four

Institutions

This photograph of Chamberlain Square in 1957 shows the old Central Library on the left; the library was completed by John Henry Chamberlain in 1882. Beside the library is Mason's College, the old university building completed by Jethro Cossins in 1880. Before them both rises the Gothic memorial fountain, designed by J.H. Chamberlain and erected in honour of Joseph Chamberlain in 1880. With the adjoining town hall and museum and art gallery, these buildings presented a stunning architectural ensemble, an embodiment of the late Victorian civic gospel that set high store on the value of local government. Of the buildings in the picture, only the fountain survived the Paradise Circus redevelopment.

The City Museum and Art Gallery, damaged by a parachute mine in 1940, needed some reconstruction following the war and the opportunity was taken to introduce modern facilities such as a café, public toilets, and a new day lighting system. There was much rearrangement and refurbishment of individual galleries. The most startling change took place in the Industrial Hall, where a false ceiling was introduced and new display cases for the ceramic and textile collections were brought in for the 1951 reopening.

This storeroom, in the upper levels of the Industrial Hall, shows something of the ornate iron vaulting that was concealed from public view through the 1950s, 1960s and 1970s; it was finally revealed again in 1984 when several galleries were fully restored.

The Museum of Science and Industry in Newhall Street, seen here in 1973, was established by the city council in 1950. It took over a factory recently vacated by Elkingtons', a long-standing electroplating company. The first galleries opened in 1951 in Elkingtons' old showrooms.

In 1953, a former workshop was transformed into the Engineering Hall (seen in 1959), containing the first working exhibits. The museum was the first in Britain to regularly display live steam engines. Many machines also worked at the touch of a button.

Young visitors admire the Ruston Proctor portable engine in 1973.

Left: In this 1975 photograph, an attendant is seen looking after one of the Science Museum's most popular exhibits, an Austin 7.

Below: Children in the Transport Hall in 1973. Although in itself a monument to Birmingham's industrial heritage, the building was closed in 1997 and most of the stock later transferred to Millennium Point.

One of the casualties of 1960s redevelopment was the Birmingham and Midland Institute in Ratcliff Place, completed by E.M. Barry in 1857. This photograph, taken in 1966 shortly before its demolition, shows the Gothic extension in Paradise Street which J.H. Chamberlain added in 1881.

The elaborate Gothic staircase also in 1966. A pioneer of adult education, with good library and club facilities, the Institute was equally at home offering a classical concert, a lecture in meteorology, or a class in Old Icelandic. Three famous Birmingham institutions, the School of Music (now the Conservatoire), Edgbaston Observatory, and the School of Art all sprang directly from it.

The Midland Institute lecture theatre in 1966. There were regular individual guest lectures, as well as special courses and conferences.

The lecturer's view of the hall in 1966 included several Neo-Gothic stained glass windows. Following demolition of the Ratcliff Place premises, the Institute combined its resources with those of the Birmingham Library in Margaret Street, to which members already had access.

Above: The central library
building in 1973, shortly
before its demolition. Built
from 1863-65 to an overall
design by E.M. Barry, with the
adjoining Midland Institute, it
formed part of a single
building extending from
Edmund Street to Paradise
Street. The interior was
completed by Martin &
Chamberlain, who were also
engaged to rebuild the library
following the fire of 1879.

Right: The library entrance hall
in 1971, with rich tiling,
wrought ironwork, and
abstract stained glass.

Above: The main reading room of the Central Reference Library, again in 1971; its vaulted ceiling, clerestory windows, soaring columns and arcades all carried ecclesiastical overtones as befits a 'temple of learning'.

Opposite above: The wing of the reference library, showing the top-lit vaulted ceiling and the intricate iron galleries. It was photographed in 1971.

Opposite below: A Central Library workroom in 1971. Like many buildings of its period, the library had fine public rooms, but cramped and inconvenient staff accommodation.

Above: The building of the new Central Library in 1973, with the old library visible to the right. There had been plans for a new building since before the war. The new library, raised on pillars above a concourse, and lit mainly by means of a central void to aid its inward-looking intention, was designed by John Madin who, with James Roberts, was responsible for much of the new post-war Birmingham construction.

Left: Reference library books were wheeled by a trolley directly from the old building to the new along a specially constructed bridge, seen here in 1973.

The demolition of the old Central Library in 1973.

The entrance to the new Central Library in 1975.

Above: This view of the Central Library and Town Hall in 1980 shows the space on the left, beneath the library, which was originally intended for a bus station, but was later converted to a bookstore. Paradise Circus follows the line of the old Ratcliff Place, with traffic passing directly beneath Chamberlain Square and the library.

Left: The Unitarian Church of the Messiah in Broad Street in 1973. Designed in the Decorated style by J.J. Bateman (1860-62) and built on arches over the Birmingham Canal, this large Gothic building reflected the importance of the Unitarians in Birmingham in the second half of the nineteenth century (when the Chamberlains and the Nettlefolds were especially prominent).

The interior of the Church of the Messiah in 1973.

The Church interior, again in 1973.

The demolition of the Church of the Messiah in 1978. This is an example of an archetypal city centre scene through the 1960s and 1970s. The church was not replaced by another building, and the site was used as a public garden, before being cleared away completely to open up a view of the restored canal. Many city centre churches were demolished at this time. Some had become redundant through declining local populations; others were in the way of road widening and were replaced elsewhere.

Like many buildings on this street, the Old Meeting Church in Bristol Street, seen here in 1954, fell victim to wholesale redevelopment after serving the area since 1885.

Wycliffe Baptist Church in Bristol Street, *c.* 1956. Like its near neighbours, the church was destined to soon disappear. It had stood here since 1861.

St Catherine of Siena Catholic church was built from 1964-65 by Harrison & Cox to replace its Victorian counterpart nearby, which had been displaced by road widening. A bright, well-proportioned building, it provides a harmonious contrast with the soaring 1970s Sentinels flats behind.

five

Events

Above: A funeral service for George VI, who died on 6 February 1952. A large crowd fills Victoria Square and closely encircles the wreaths surrounding Queen Victoria's statue.

Opposite below: Christmas decorations surround Queen Victoria's statue in 1967.

Above: The decorations outside the Town Hall honour a visit made by Queen Elizabeth in 1955.

MUSEUM OF SCIENCE AND INDUSTRY
Newhall Street. Birmingham. B3 1RZ

STEAM WEEK-END

This Beam Engine, together with many
other forms of Steam Engine,
can be seen working on live steam on

SATURDAY and SUNDAY

NOVEMBER 20th & 21st 1976

Steam weekends were a popular event at the old Museum of Science and Industry for many years; stationary engines frequently performed indoors while mobile engines operated outside.

The Birmingham & District Theatre Guild

THEATRE ROYAL   BIRMINGHAM

Commemoration Dinner

Imperial Hotel

Saturday, December 15th, 1956

THEATRE ROYAL 1774

Right: The Birmingham and District Theatre Guild held a commemorative dinner at the Imperial Hotel on 15 December 1956 to mark the passing of the Theatre Royal, the city's oldest and most famous theatre, soon to be replaced by Woolworths (now themselves replaced).

Below: A visit by local schoolchildren to Gas Street Basin in 1978. The city centre canals have become an increasingly important educational resource following their steady regeneration during the past three decades.

Last Night of the Proms in Birmingham Town Hall in 1974.

A BBC *Come Dancing* contest at the Locarno Ballroom in Hurst Street, *c.* 1960.

The scene following the IRA bombing of the Tavern in the Town in New Street on 20 November 1974.

The scene following the bombing of the Mulberry Bush beneath the Rotunda on 20 November 1974.

Left: A fire at the King's Hall market in 1962. Originally a nonconformist church, it served as a cinema for some years before its conversion to a market hall in the early 1920s.

Below: A fire at Lewis's warehouse in 1973.

Above: A Liberal
conference at the Council
House in 1975.

Left: The Italian Festival
(1974) hosts an open-air
concert in Chamberlain
Square; it shows the
semi-circular
amphitheatre in front of
the new central library
being put to good use.

Above: When the redeveloped Chamberlain Square was laid out in the early 1970s, it was envisaged that the steep, wide steps leading to the new library would provide a ready-made auditorium for a great variety of events. This photograph depicts one such event, a polytechnic student demonstration against public spending cuts, in 1974

Left: The Parks Department's floral sculpture of the World Cup, won by England in 1966, is displayed in Victoria Square with Galloway's Corner and one of the then ubiquitous Lyons Cafés in the background.

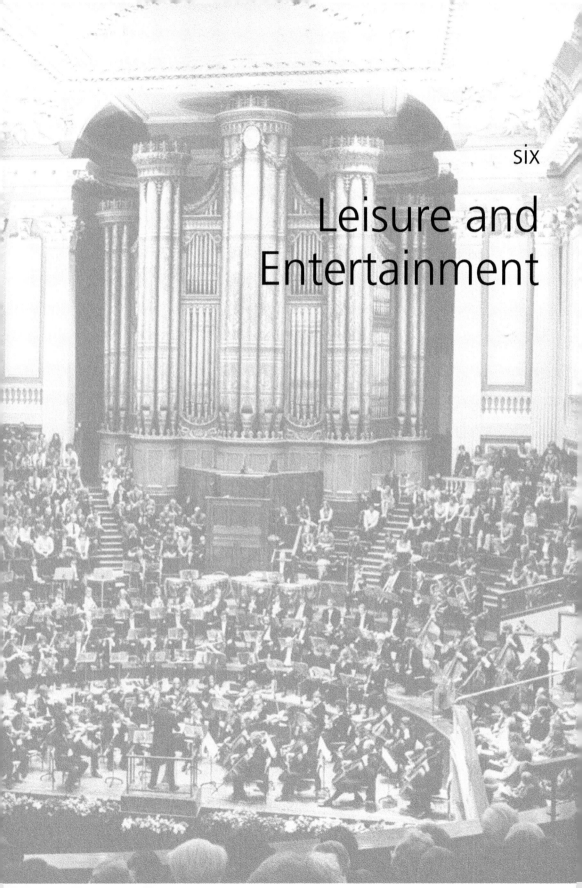

six

Leisure and Entertainment

St Philip's Cathedral churchyard, seen here in around 1958, has long been a place of rest and relaxation for shoppers and office workers in the summer.

Right: Shoppers relax in a newly pedestrianized area of the High Street in 1973.

Below: The Grand Hotel from the churchyard in 1979. Completed in 1875 by J.A. Chatwin, it was remodelled by Martin and Chamberlain in 1891. For much of the twentieth century, it remained one of the city's leading traditional hotels with an ornate vaulted assembly room used for a great variety of meetings. It recently ceased to function as a hotel but is now a listed building and is currently awaiting a new use.

Although parts of central Birmingham were ripe for redevelopment, being run-down or bomb-damaged, the loss of some buildings in the Easy Row and Edmund Street area (now Paradise Circus) was regretted. One such loss was the White Horse Hotel at the junction of Great Charles Street and Congreve Street. Rebuilt by Wood and Kendrick in 1906, it was a popular meeting place, with well-used function rooms for many years. In the photograph taken in 1965, its panelled restaurant with ornate plaster ceiling awaits demolition to make way for a new road and library.

Among the saddest losses to the Paradise Circus development was the Woodman on Easy Row, rebuilt in 1891 on the site of a former coaching inn to the design of Henry Naden. This Public Works photograph, taken shortly before the building's demolition in 1964, shows the elaborate triple-doored entrance (above which stood a life-size statue of a woodman in an alcove).

This view of the private bar of the Woodman on the same occasion shows the snob-screens, ornate woodcarving and painted windows.

As can be seen in this 1964 photograph, the smoke-room of the Woodman had an intricate wooden alcove around the fireplace. Even the public bar had many large tiled murals depicting local scenes. The pub remained remarkably unaltered until its closure and today would have been appreciated by visitors to the city. Commemorated by nearby Fletcher's Walk (named after a former landlord), it was undoubtedly the finest of several notable Victorian pubs lost to 1960s redevelopment.

Left: Another Public Works Department photograph shows the Victoria on Bristol Street in 1964, shortly before the whole of this side of the road was demolished to create a dual carriageway. This street lost several old pubs, including the Bell, Nottingham Arms, Red Cow, and Sun.

Below: The Silver Blades Ice Rink at the junction of Hurst Street and Bromsgrove Street in 1972.

Above: The closure of the Theatre Royal in New Street on 15 December 1956, shortly before this picture was taken, marked the end of an era. Tracing its origins back to 1774, and described by Birmingham historian William Hutton as 'one of the finest theatres in the world', over the years, it played host to many of the major stars. In its final form, following a 1904 rebuilding, it achieved a legendary reputation under director Philip Rodway, who was especially noted for his musical performances.

Right: The annual Theatre Royal pantomime was eagerly awaited by successive generations of patrons, having been performed here at least as early as 1796. *Old King Cole* was staged in 1955-56.

Above: The auditorium of the Theatre Royal in 1956.

Left: The final show at the theatre was a musical revue, The Fol-de-Rols. Remarkably, no mention was made of the impending closure in the programme although an emotional farewell was taken by actors and audience at the final performance. The Woolworths building later occupied the site.

Opposite below: The new foyer of the Alexandra (seen in 1975) was built in 1968 to bridge John Bright Street and link the theatre directly to the Ring Road. Opened in 1901 and rebuilt in 1935, the 'Alex' was run for many years by the Salberg family and staged regular repertory performances from 1927 to 1974. The main auditorium in the original building on John Bright Street was recently extensively refurbished.

Above: The new Repertory Theatre on Broad Street is seen in 1978 from its then extensive and attractive front gardens. Started on Station Street in 1913 by Sir Barry Jackson for his amateur Pilgrim Players (who later turned professional), it was the first theatre to be built for repertory purposes, and it became the training ground for many future stars. The new theatre was opened in 1971 with more than twice the seating capacity of its predecessor, (it seated 901 people, whereas it had originally only seated 450) and a studio for 120. Well-lit, well-equipped bars and restaurants occupied the concourse areas fronting the auditorium which was raked without galleries.

The West End Cinema in Suffolk Street in 1957. Formerly Curzon Hall (an exhibition centre), from 1925 it offered not only a cinema but also a popular restaurant and dance hall. It was closed in 1967 and subsequently demolished to make way for the Inner Ring Road.

The Futurist Cinema in John Bright Street opened in 1919 with seating for 1,245 people. Seen from Hill Street in 1972, it was the first Birmingham cinema to show a 'talkie' (Al Jolson's *The Singing Fool*) in 1929. Bombed in 1940, it reopened in 1943 and became a two-screen cinema in 1981. It is now a nightclub.

Above: The Scala Cinema, shown in 1956, with parts of Smallbrook Street already demolished, opened in 1914 with seating for 800. It was a luxurious cinema noted for its orchestra in the early days. It closed in 1960 and was demolished soon afterwards as Smallbrook Street became the Ringway.

Right: The Albany Hotel and the rebuilt Scala Cinema, looking up Smallbrook Ringway towards the Bull Ring, *c.* 1971. The Albany Hotel was built in 1962 by James Roberts. Later the Post House Hotel, it was the first to be built in the city centre since the turn of the century. James Roberts also completed Scala House in 1964; Scala House included offices and the new cinema which is now closed.

The Delicia Cinema in Gosta Green opened in 1923 and closed as a cinema in 1946. At the time of this photograph (1951), it had been converted to a boxing and wrestling venue. It later served as a BBC television studio and as part of the Triangle Arts Centre. More recently, it became a bookshop.

The interior of the Delicia in 1951 showing the boxing and wrestling ring.

Above: A CBSO concert at the Town Hall in 1978.

Right: A Royal Marine band at the Town Hall in 1975.

An open-air performance for the Italian Festival in Chamberlain Square in 1974.

Morris men dancing in the Central Library concourse with the Art Gallery in the background in 1975. The concourse was later roofed and glazed, becoming the Forum, comprising a group of shops, bars and restaurants.

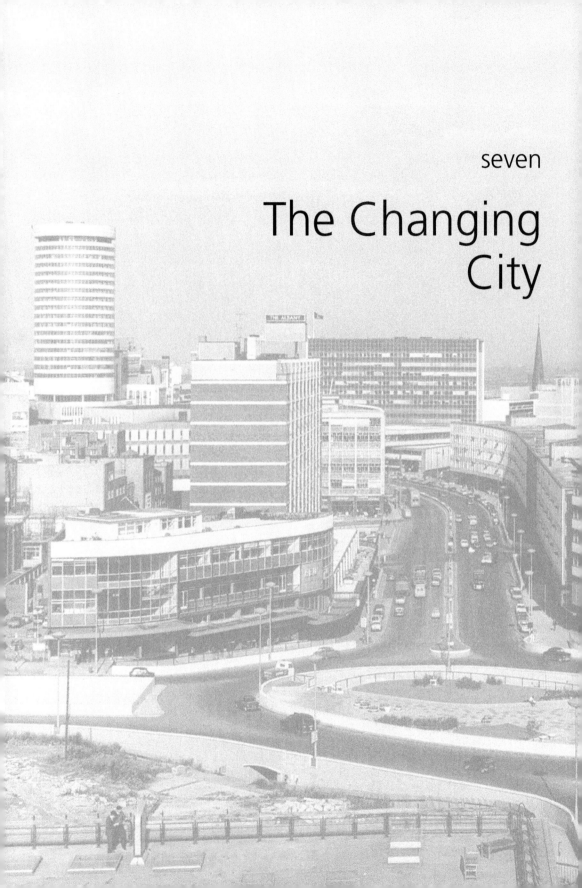

seven

The Changing City

Above: An aerial view of the city centre taken in 1963. In this essentially transitional scene, the original New Street station is still seen in operation, just before the cranes and bulldozers move in. To the left of the station stands the tall narrow form of the Queen's Hotel, then one of Birmingham's best-known old-established venues. Beyond New Street station rises the almost completed Rotunda, like the hub of a wheel, with the partly completed Bull Ring on its right, its rectangular blocks already beginning to hem in St Martin's church. To the bottom left of the picture, work is already beginning on the new station signal box, and there are signs of earlier post-war developments including the 1950s Woolworths building (towards the bottom left), and the Big Top Centre (to the left of the Rotunda). The triangular bulk of the newly finished Bull Ring bus station rises to the right of the railway station.

Opposite below: An aerial view of Masshouse Circus in 1972. This was one of the Inner Ring Road's seven main junctions with incoming arterial roads and a large traffic island – in this case raised on stilts. The character of the Ring Road is immediately apparent – designed primarily as a traffic road with few shop, office or warehouse frontages. Traffic and pedestrians are successfully separated but the 'concrete collar' discourages people from going beyond the Ring Road. Masshouse Circus suffered from 'planning blight', the area immediately around it never being more than a car park. It has now been demolished to improve access to the Eastside.

Above: An aerial view of Gas Street Basin and the city centre taken in 1975 shows most of the old canal buildings still intact. There is a mixture of old and new on the left, with high-rise blocks and the new Repertory Theatre vying for attention with the dark bulk of Bingley Hall, which is the site of the present ICC. Most of Broad Street's old buildings still remain at this time, but there are signs of things to come: the new Central Library is to the right of the photograph, at the rear, and Alpha Tower is the tall building on the right, on the site of the demolished West End Chambers.

Above: In 1974, a building site carpenter looks out over the new Birmingham he is helping to create. In the foreground are St Philip's Cathedral and the Waterloo Street and Colmore Row business quarter, still substantially unaltered. Beyond the cathedral churchyard, however, are recent redevelopments, including the new Bank of England building rising in the centre of the picture and, on either side and just behind it, the Martineau Square and Big Top shopping centres. The Rotunda rises on the right, already becoming a monomark of modern Birmingham.

Opposite above: The Inner Ring Road plan was first discussed as early as 1917. A one-way traffic system was introduced in 1933, becoming the butt of comedians for its complexity. The Ring Road plans were approved by Parliament in 1944, but were held back by lack of capital for twelve years. Meanwhile, 85 acres of land and 1,200 buildings were compulsorily purchased in preparation. As the map shows, Colmore Row was originally envisaged as part of the scheme, but conservationists succeeded in blocking this. The plan shows the new road cutting through existing street patterns, much as Victorian railways did.

Opposite below: Construction work on the underpass from High Street to the Bull Ring in 1959 – a scene characteristic of the period, which prompted more than one commentator to speak of a second blitz. At this early stage of reconstruction, the old and the new still co-existed, the walls of the roofless Market Hall rising on the right still sheltering an open market (as they would until 1962).

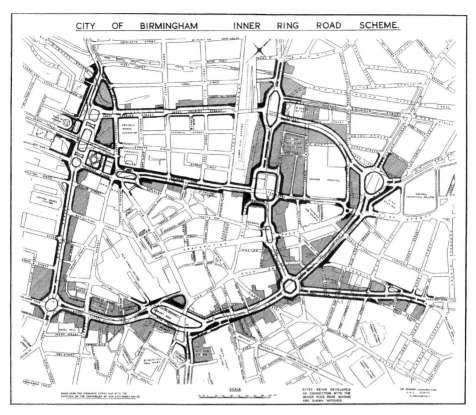

CITY OF BIRMINGHAM INNER RING ROAD SCHEME.

SCALE

BASED UPON THE ORDNANCE SURVEY MAP WITH THE
SANCTION OF THE CONTROLLER OF H.M. STATIONERY OFFICE.

SITES BEING DEVELOPED
IN CONNECTION WITH THE
INNER RING ROAD SCHEME
ARE SHOWN HATCHED

SIR HERBERT J MANZONI C.B.E.
CIVIC CENTRE
BIRMINGHAM I.

Left: Snow Hill before redevelopment in 1959.

Below: Snow Hill in 1964, totally cleared to make way for the Inner Ring Road. St Chad's Cathedral now stands, prominently isolated, where it once rose above narrow streets of terraced housing. The right-hand side of the road beside Snow Hill station was never rebuilt, and remains a car park to this day.

Opposite above: Work proceeds on the Ring Road beside St Chad's Cathedral in 1961. The Gun Quarter (lying straight ahead) was bisected by the new road and many Georgian properties of varying quality were demolished.

Above: The Inner Ring Road was completed in 1971, fourteen years after its official inauguration. Here may be seen St Chad's Circus in 1972 with the Cathedral rising above one of several pedestrian subways enlivened by murals, in this case on the themes of J.F. Kennedy and Snow Hill Station.

Emerging from a pedestrian subway beneath St Chad's Circus, c. 1972. This is an archetypal image of the new city built round the Ring Road. The fifty-two subways were initially popular, seen as novel and convenient, though from the start satirists wrote of troglodyte dwellings and there were cartoons featuring cavemen. Many subways did not wear well, however, and became dark, squalid and threatening within a few years. Within twenty years, the process was being reversed; in Paradise Circus, for example, the road was lowered and a pedestrian bridge raised above it.

Demolition work in Smallbrook Street in 1956. It was perhaps appropriate that the Inner Ring Road should be started here since much of the property was run down and there were several unreclaimed bomb sites. As leases expired, compulsory purchase orders were issued, and the buildings were quickly pulled down.

More demolition work on Smallbrook Street in 1956. Here, scaffolding already surrounds the premises of George Hull the drysalter, oil, varnish and paint manufacturer.

Smallbrook Ringway (later Queensway) of 1966 was a striking, uncompromisingly modern improvement on the preceding street. Its design was clearly influenced by the ideas of the Swiss architect Le Corbusier, a pioneer of 'total plans' for cities, who envisaged new developments arising, phoenix-like, from the ashes of their hide-bound past. Its fresh, radical nature was emphasised by the red road surface which it originally boasted. Smallbrook Ringway was the only part of the Ring Road to be planned as a mainstream shopping centre, although ironically it never fully achieved this status being insufficiently 'central' and, until recently, needing to be reached on the south side by one of its own subways. It does, however, retain some good specialist shops and its accessibility has now been much improved by lowering the road surface and replacing the subway with a pedestrian crossing.

Opposite below: Old Square subway in 1975 shows more ambitious shopping facilities surrounding an open-air square with seating, used occasionally for entertainments such as folk dancing. Small public gardens within a traffic island became a feature of the post-war city, other examples appearing within St Chad's Circus, Holloway Circus and St Martin's Circus (Manzoni Gardens). In 1998 the Old Square's 'hole' was filled in and the pedestrian route restored to ground level as part of the plan to open up Eastside and Millennium Point.

Above: The Hill Street subway running beneath Smallbrook Ringway was Britain's first pedestrian subway, and generated many imitations in other towns and cities. Seen here in 1961, it was of higher status than many in that it had various facilities including shops, telephone kiosks and public conveniences as well as being wide and well lit. Like the others, it came to be seen as a barrier between the city centre and the streets beyond – in this case the important entertainment quarter centring on Hurst Street.

Great Charles Street in 1971, shortly after the official opening of the Ring Road (or Queensway) by the Queen. The tunnels pass through Great Charles Street's hilly southern end and beneath Paradise Circus to emerge in Suffolk Street. Similar engineering challenges were met at St Chad's Circus, with a tunnel link to Aston Expressway.

Suffolk Street in 1979 showing how the Great Charles Street tunnel passes beneath the School of Music and the Central Library beyond it. Alpha Tower rises on the left from the site of the old canal basin and close to where the old West End Cinema once stood (see page 102).

Demolition work progresses as Paradise Street prepares for the Inner Ring Road in 1965.

Old and new meet on Paradise Street in 1961 before the widening of Suffolk Street on the right.

Above: Building the Suffolk Street footbridge in 1971.

Left: Work progresses in Corporation Street in 1963 in preparation for what became known as the 'Bull Street hump', an artificially created hill enclosing subways linking the two parts of Corporation Street and Bull Street. Lewis's store had their own subterranean departments here: a record store, a bread and cake shop, a gentleman's outfitters and a coffee bar. All of these vanished in 2000 when the hump was lowered and the subway filled in, partly to help pedestrians, and partly to ease the passage of the proposed Metro tram.

Opposite below: Work on the Holloway Circus underpass in 1964. Old faces new across this part of Suffolk Street, with demolition of the right-hand side of Bristol Street under way straight ahead in order to create a dual carriageway.

Work progresses in 1965 on the tunnels beneath Holloway Circus, an underpass beneath a roundabout foreshadowing the larger and later Five Ways layout. On the lawn within the roundabout a reclining statue of Hebe, the goddess of youth and spring, was placed; this marked the site of the first ceremonial demolition, launching the Inner Ring Road project. On the horizon, scaffolding still clings to the Post Office Tower, soon to be Birmingham's tallest building at 500ft.

Photographed in 1955, these houses in Smithfield Passage, in the market area, are a reminder of how many ordinary people lived on that side of the city centre into quite recent times.

In 1973, the ball and chain are already at work on Sherlock Street and Jamaica Row, the latter soon to vanish beneath the new wholesale markets complex.

The old wholesale markets await their fate in 1973 with new pipes already lined up in readiness for the new development.

Construction work on the Five Ways underpass in 1970.

Above: Aerial view of Lancaster Circus and Aston Expressway in 1972 looking towards the city centre. In the background, the Central Hall and Law Courts rise on the left, the General Hospital and Dental Hospital straight ahead and the spires of St Chad's Cathedral and St Paul's Church on the right.

Opposite above: Constructing the Lancaster Circus flyover with the University of Aston in the background in 1970.

Opposite below: Beneath the Lancaster Circus flyover with Halfords to the left, in 1971, shortly after completion of the Inner Ring Road. This was the last section to be finished. Halford's is now the present site of council offices.

This view of Masshouse Circus under construction in 1965 shows how the Inner Ring Road, here on stilts, cut a great swathe through surrounding properties. The old Beehive store clings on to the left, while Aston university closes the view just beyond. The road has recently been lowered to ground level again, to provide direct access to Eastside.

Bath Row before redevelopment in 1960.

A transitional scene in Lee Bank near Bath Row during redevelopment in 1957.

New flats at Bell Barn Road in Lee Bank in 1959. Lee Bank (now Attwood Green) was one of the five inner suburbs chosen for comprehensive redevelopment. At the time, the new housing, with its modern facilities and green, open setting, seemed in striking contrast to the run-down, confined courts and terraces it had replaced, and a documentary film was made about the area. Forty-five years later, a further phase of rebuilding is being implemented here as the city adapts itself once again to ever-changing needs.